First World War
and Army of Occupation
War Diary
France, Belgium and Germany

27 DIVISION
81 Infantry Brigade
Princess Louise's (Argyll & Sutherland Highlanders)
1/9th Battalion
18 February 1915 - 30 April 1915

WO95/2263/3

The Naval & Military Press Ltd
www.nmarchive.com
Published in association with The National Archives

Published by

The Naval & Military Press Ltd

Unit 10 Ridgewood Industrial Park,

Uckfield, East Sussex,

TN22 5QE England

Tel: +44 (0) 1825 749494

www.naval-military-press.com

www.nmarchive.com

This diary has been reprinted in facsimile from the original. Any imperfections are inevitably reproduced and the quality may fall short of modern type and cartographic standards.

© **Crown Copyright**
Images reproduced by permission of The National Archives, London, England, 2015.

Contents

Document type	Place/Title	Date From	Date To
Heading	WO95/2263-3		
Heading	9th Bn Argyll & Suth'd Hdrs Mar-Apr 1915		
Heading	1/9th Battn, The Argyll & Sutherland Highlanders. February (18 to 28.2.15) 1915		
War Diary	Bedford	18/02/1915	18/02/1915
War Diary	Southampton	19/02/1915	19/02/1915
War Diary	Havre	20/02/1915	22/02/1915
War Diary	Cassel	23/02/1915	23/02/1915
War Diary	St Marie Capel	24/02/1915	26/02/1915
War Diary	St Marie Capel-Mt Kokerele	27/02/1915	27/02/1915
War Diary	Mt. Kokerele	28/02/1915	28/02/1915
Heading	1/9th Battn. The Argyll & Sutherland Highlanders March 1915		
War Diary	Mt Kokerele	01/03/1915	06/03/1915
War Diary	Rosenhill	07/03/1915	15/03/1915
War Diary	Dickebusch	16/03/1915	22/03/1915
War Diary	Mt Kokerele	23/03/1915	25/03/1915
War Diary	Ypres	26/03/1915	31/03/1915
Heading	War Diary of 9th Argyll And Sutherland Highlanders From February 18th 1915 to March 31st 1915		
Miscellaneous		12/03/1915	12/03/1915
Miscellaneous	1/9th Battn. Arg. & Sutherland Highlanders.	20/03/1915	20/03/1915
Miscellaneous	1/9th Battn. Arg. & Suthl. Highlanders.	23/03/1915	23/03/1915
Miscellaneous	1/9th Bn. Arg. & Suth. Highlrs.		
Miscellaneous	1/9th Battalion Arg. & Sutherland Highlanders.	26/03/1915	26/03/1915
Miscellaneous	1/9th Battn Arg. & Sutherland Highlanders.	30/03/1915	30/03/1915
Miscellaneous	1/9th Bn. Argyll & Sutherland Highlanders.	31/03/1915	31/03/1915
Miscellaneous	Casualties Affecting Officers		
Heading	1/9th Battn. The Argyll & Sutherland Highlanders. April 1915		
War Diary	Ypres	01/04/1915	04/04/1915
War Diary	Herelhaqe	05/04/1915	08/04/1915
War Diary	Vlamertinghe	09/04/1915	12/04/1915
War Diary	Glencorse Wood	13/04/1915	16/04/1915
War Diary	Ypres	17/04/1915	20/04/1915
War Diary	Gleucorse Wood	21/04/1915	30/04/1915
Miscellaneous	Command Paymaster, Rouen.	02/04/1915	02/04/1915
Miscellaneous	1/9th Battalion Argyll & Sutherland Hrs.	03/04/1915	03/04/1915
Miscellaneous	1/9th Battn Arg & Suthld Highlrs.	07/04/1915	07/04/1915
Miscellaneous	1/9th Battalion Argyll & Suth Hrs.	15/04/1915	15/04/1915
Miscellaneous	1/9th Battn. Argyll & Suth Highrs.	17/04/1915	17/04/1915
Miscellaneous	1/9th Battn. Argyll & Suth Hrs.	20/04/1915	20/04/1915
Miscellaneous	1/9th Battn. Argyll & Suthd Hrs.	23/04/1915	23/04/1915

WO95/22631/3

27TH DIVISION
81ST INFY BDE

9TH BN ARGYLL & SUTH'D HDRS

~~FEB~~ - APR 1915
MAR

(To 10 Bde 4 Div.
AMALGAMATED WITH 7 BN) OK

~~TO 6 CORPS TROOPS~~

81st Inf. Bde.
27th Div.

Battn. disembarked
Havre from England
20.2.15.

1/9th BATTN. THE ARGYLL & SUTHERLAND HIGHLANDERS.

F E B R U A R Y

(18 to 28.2.15)

1 9 1 5

WAR DIARY or INTELLIGENCE SUMMARY.

Army Form C. 2118.

(Erase heading not required.)

Instructions regarding War Diaries and Intelligence Summaries are contained in F. S. Regs., Part II. and the Staff Manual respectively. Title pages will be prepared in manuscript.

Place	Date	Hour	Summary of Events and Information	Remarks and references to Appendices
BEDFORD	Feb. 18.		Orders received to move to SOUTHAMPTON.	
SOUTHAMPTON	19.	3 a.m. 6.15 a.m. 8 a.m. 4.30 p.m. 6.15 p.m.	Left BEDFORD. Embarks at SOUTHAMPTON on "Empress Queen". ½ Bn. AT Cameroud on board ARCHIMEDES. Sailed 6.15 p.m. Transport with personnel on board ARCHIMEDES.	
HAVRE	20.	1 a.m. 7 a.m. 8.30 a.m.	Arrived in harbour. No orders received to disembark till 7 a.m. Disembarked. Rations issued on Quay. Marched 8.30 a.m. to No 6 Rest Camp. Sizes sent in at once for all deficiencies. Transport arrived in camp at midnight.	
HAVRE	21st.		Articles indented for received – Inspection by Camp Commandant – Other recommendations for Entraining at 8 a.m. following morning	
HAVRE	22nd	2.30 a.m. 7.30 a.m.	Arrived Station 2.30 a.m. Train moved off at 7.30 a.m. The long wait at Station caused inconvenience Men 37 per cattle truck.	
CASSEL	23rd	6.45 a.m.	Arrived CASSEL 6.45 a.m. – Detrained – marched ST. MARIE CAPEL. Learnt that the Batton formed part of 81st Brigade – 27th Division.	
ST.MARIE CAPEL	24th		A man sent to ST. OMER for Course of Cold Shoeing –	
ST.MARIE CAPEL	25th		Inspected by Gen. Sir H. SMITH DORIEN. – Received orders to move to BOESCHEPE on 27th inst.	

Army Form C. 2118.

WAR DIARY
or
INTELLIGENCE SUMMARY.
(Erase heading not required.)

Instructions regarding War Diaries and Intelligence Summaries are contained in F. S. Regs., Part II. and the Staff Manual respectively. Title pages will be prepared in manuscript.

Place	Date	Hour	Summary of Events and Information	Remarks and references to Appendices
	Feb.			
ST. MARIE CAPEL	26th		19 miners under Lieut. STEWART despatched to C.R.E. 27th Div. RENINGHELST.	
ST. MARIE CAPEL - MT KOKERELE	27th		Proceeded by march route to MOUNT KOKERELE van BOESCHEPE via CASSEL - ABEELE.	
MT. KOKERELE	28th		Visit by Brig. Genl. 81st Brigade. Capt. YOUNG 1st ARGYLLS attached to motor.	

1577 Wt. W10791/1773 500,000 1/15 D. D. & L. A.D.S.S./Form/C. 2118.

81st Inf.Bde.
27th Div.

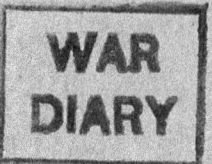

1/9th BATTN. THE ARGYLL & SUTHERLAND HIGHLANDERS.

M A R C H

1 9 1 5

WAR DIARY or INTELLIGENCE SUMMARY.

(Erase heading not required.)

Instructions regarding War Diaries and Intelligence Summaries are contained in F. S. Regs., Part II. and the Staff Manual respectively. Title pages will be prepared in manuscript.

Place	Date	Hour	Summary of Events and Information	Remarks and references to Appendices
MT KOKERELE	MARCH 1st		Nil.	
MT KOKERELE	2nd		Inspected by Brig. Gen. MACFARLANE Comdg. 81st Brigade. 8 Signallers attached Brigade Headquarters for instruction.	
MT KOKERELE	3rd		Tested Rifles of A and B Companies. Min fires after 1st Test. E } 81.	
MT KOKERELE	4th		Tested Rifles of C and D Companies. Min fires after 1st Test. After overhauling by Armourer Sergt. Retested rifles of A & B Companies. Others received to despatch 2 Platoons & 2 Sections to 80th Brigade as carrying party unfollowing day.	
MT KOKERELE	5th		Retested rifles of C & D Companies after overhauling by Armourer Sergt. Total mis-fires after 2nd Test 15. 2 Platoons attached 80th Brigade proceeded to huts behind DICKEBUSCH.	
MT KOKERELE	6th		Billeting party despatched to take over huts at ROSENHILL.	
MT KOKERELE ROSENHILL	7th		Proceeded by march route to huts at ROSENHILL. 2 casualties in Platoon attached 80th Brigade. Brig. Gen. MACFARLANE visited the Bn. at ROSENHILL and arranged that 2 Platoons from 2 Companies should (without Lt. Turner, lately commanding on 6th inst.) proceed after (briefing?) exchange at ordnance 27 & 2-15.	
ROSENHILL	8th		O.C. Snowy Comdg. 27th Bn. visited Camp. 2 Platoons from B Company and 2 Platoons from "C" proceeded to DICKEBUSCH and came attached to 1 MARQUILLES 2nd Canadians.	

INTELLIGENCE SUMMARY.

(Erase heading not required.)

Place	Date	Hour	Summary of Events and Information	Remarks and references to Appendices
ROSENHILL	MARCH 9th		2 Platoons from B and C Companies proceeded to DICKEBUSCH and were attached to 2nd GLOUCESTERS Regt. 1st ROYAL SCOTS inspected. 2 Platoons of "A" Coy. ordered to perform duties of carrying up to trenches. Gen. SIR H. PLUMER visited the camp.	
ROSENHILL	10th		4 Platoons of "D" Coy. proceeded to DICKEBUSCH and were attached 2 Platoons to 2nd GLOUCESTERS and 2 Platoons to 1st ROYAL SCOTS 24 hours in trenches. 3 Casualties, O.R. wounded.	
ROSENHILL	11th		Company attacked 80th Brigade Since 5th relieved and with the other 2 Platoons of "A" Coy proceeded to DICKEBUSCH and were attached to 1st ARGYLLS and 2nd CAMERONS 24 hours in trenches.	
ROSENHILL	12th		One Casualty during relief.	
ROSENHILL	14th		Orders to "Stand by" received at 7.15 p.m. owing to German attack on St ELOI.	
ROSENHILL	15th		Standing by.	
ROSENHILL DICKEBUSCH	16th		Remainder of march into DICKEBUSCH. B & C Coys were attached to ARGYLLS & CAMERONS from 12 noon till 12 noon 24 hours. 5 Casualties, 1 OR wounded.	

INTELLIGENCE SUMMARY.

(Erase heading not required.)

Place	Date	Hour	Summary of Events and Information	Remarks and references to Appendices
DICKEBUSCH	March 18		A and D Coys relieved B and C in the Trenches. 3 casualties.	
DICKEBUSCH	19th		A and D Coys relieved. 3 casualties.	
DICKEBUSCH	21st		500 men employed on digging on the 2nd line in the St Eloi Section. 3 casualties. Shell landed in farm where D Coy was billeted. 1 officer and 3 O.R. wounded.	
DICKEBUSCH	22nd		500 men employed on a [?] a 2nd line in St Eloi section. 5 casualties	
DICKEBUSCH MT KOKERELE	23rd		Proceeded by march route to MT KOKERELE arrived 11.30 p.m.	
MT KOKERELE	25th		Inspection of the Battn. by Brig. Gl. CROKER ordered received about 9 p.m. to proceed to YPRES a following morning.	
YPRES	26th		The Battn proceeded by march route [via WESTOUTRE - RENINGHELST - VLAMARTINGHE] to YPRES. Arrived about midday [no billets had been arranged in the Batton walked 2 hours before moving off to their billets]. Patrol of 150 men sent about 1/2 mile outside line south of PORTE DE LILLE.	

INTELLIGENCE SUMMARY.

(Erase heading not required.)

Place	Date	Hour	Summary of Events and Information	Remarks and references to Appendices
YPRES	27th		Major CHRISTIE and the four Cav[alry] Commandants and three NCO's went up to the Frontier of the French 17th Div. for purpose of reconnaissance and selecting a new Frontier. New ground following down. 500 men sent to dig on 2nd line S. of PORTE DE LILLE. Party of 500 men to dig on 2nd line.	
YPRES	28th			
YPRES	29th		Orders received to despatch an officer to ROUEN to fetch draft of 70 men from Res. Bat[talio]n. Lieut STEWART sent for this purpose. Party of 500 sent to dig on 2nd line.	
YPRES	30th		Some cooks arrived in lieu of cooks we gave from Squadron kept armed. Party of 500 sent to dig on 2nd line.	
YPRES	31st		Our next draft of horses arrived to complete establishment. Party of 500 sent to dig on 2nd line.	

James Lloyd Lt[.] Adj[.]
A/Major 9th O.R.J. Hrs

Confidential

War Diary

of

9th Argyll and Sutherland Highlanders

from February 18th 1915 to March 31st 1915

1/9█. Battn. Arg. & █th █igh█nders.

2673 Pte. Thomson	J.	ABSCESS C.T. NECK. Ad. 6 S.H. 21/2/15.	O.C. 6 S.H.	Nil.
1735 Pte. Sherwood	G.	BRONCHITIS. To England per H.S. Nevasa. 4/3/15 Ex. 6 S.H.	O.C. 6 S.H.	Nil.
1637 Pte. Fogo	J.	DIARRHOAE. Ad. Hosp.(R.P.B. G.H.) 1/3/15	O.C. Rawal P. Brit. G.H.	Nil.

To be retd.

Captain,

12/3/1915.   I/c. Infantry Records, 3rd. Echelon, G.H.Q.

Casualties.

No.1 District.

1/9th. Battn. Arg. & Sutherland Highlanders.

Regl. No.	Rank & Name	Casualty	Rpd. by.	Prev. Rpd. Casualty.
1705	Pte. Robertson J.	NYY.D. Ad. 3 G.H. 4/3/15.	O.C. 3 G.H.	Nil.
2095	Pte. Reid W.	CONJUNCTIVITIS. Ad. 8 G.H. 7/3/15.	O.C. 8 G.H.	Nil.
1425	Drmr. Cairns H.	DEBILITY. Ad. 8 Clg. H. 4/3/15. Trand. to 10 G.H. 7/3/15	O.C. 8 Clg. H.	Nil.
361	L.Cpl. Moffatt J.	DEBILITY. Ad. 8 Clg. H. 6/3/15 Trans. to 10 A.T. 7/3/15. To Duty 12/3/15.	O.C. 8 Clg. H.	Nil.
2291	Pte. McFadyen J.	SPRAINED ANKLE LEFT. Ad. 2 S.H. 10/3/15.	O.C. 2 S.H.	Nil.
1967	Pte. Macnab W.	To Duty 11/3/15	O.C. Details Havre	S.
1393	L.Cpl. Logan M.	G.S.W. L. ARM. Ad. 10 G.H. 14/3/15.	O.C. 10 G.H.	Nil.
1573	Pte. Thomson C.	FROST BITE FEET. Ad. 9 G.H. 15/3/15. To Duty 18/3/15	O.C. 9 G.H.	Nil.
2945	Pte. McHugh J.	MUMPS. Ad. 14 S.H. 8/3/15	O.C. 14 S.H.	Nil.

Captain,

20/3/15.

I/c., Infantry Records, 3rd. Echelin, G.H.Q.

To be returned.

Casualties.

No. 1 District.

1/9th. Battn. Arg. & Suthl. Highlanders.

Regl. No.	Rank & Name	Casualty	Rpd. By.	Prev. Rpd. Casualty.
2673	Pte. Thomson J.	To Duty 14/3/15	O.C. Inf. Depot Rouen Havre	S.
2254	L.Cpl. Brown D.M.	SPRAINED ANKLE. Ad. 83rd. F.A. 9/3/15	O.C. 81 F.A.	Nil.
298	L.Cpl. McMallum W.	B.W. L. SHOULDER. Ad. 81st. F.A. 19/3/15	O.C. 81st. F.A.	nil.
2969	Pte. Larkins W.	BOMB WOUND. L. BUTTOCK Ad. 83rd. F.A. 11/3/15	O.C. 83rd. F.A.	nil.
1542	Pte. Robertson F.	CARIOUS TEETH. Ad. 83rd. F.A. 11/3/15	O.C. 83rd. F.A.	Nil.

Captain,

23/3/1915   I/c., Infantry Records, 3rd. Echelon, G.H.Q.

CASUALTIES. &No.1 District.

1/9th Bn ARG.&. SUTH.HIGHLRS.

Regtl.No.	Rank & Name.		Casualty.	By whom reported	Prev.Rpt.
1603	Pte. McQuire	J.	DIARRHOEA. Ad. 83rd. F.A. 11/3/15.	O.C. 83rd. F.A.	Nil.
96	Cpl. Brown	S.M.	B.W.L.ARM. Ad. 83rd. F.A. 13/3/15.	do.	Nil.
1767	Pte. McLean	A.	GONORRHOEA. Ad. 81st. F.A. 10/3/15.	O.C. 81st. F.A.	Nil.
1860	Pte. Allan	T.	G.S.W.BOTH BEGS. DIED OF WOUNDS 20/3/15.	O.C. 8 C.C. Stn.	Nil.

==

Hockington Captain,
I/c., Infantry Records, 3rd. Echelon, G.H.Q. 24/3/1915

CASUALTIES.   NO 1 District.

1/9th Battalion Argll & Sutherland Highlanders

Regtl. No Rank & Name	Casualty	By whom reported	Prev. Rept
1656 Pte. Condie W.	TONSOLITIS. Adm. 83rd Field Amb. 9/3/15.	O.C. 83rd Field Amb.	Nil.
1853 Pte. Anderson D.	RHEUMATISM Adm. 83rd Field Amb. 9/3/15.	do	Nil.
1796 Pte. McNiven A.	INFLAMED GUMS Adm. 83rd Field Amb. 9/3/15.	do	Nil.
283 Dr. Young J.	IMPETIGO SCALP Adm. 83rd Field Amb. 9/3/15.	do	Nil.
1326 Pte. Scott J.	RHEUMATISM & SORE GUMS. Adm. 83rd Field Amb. 9/3/15	do	Nil.
2648 Pte. Brown J.C.	D.A.H. Adm. 82nd Bde. Hospl. 7/3/15.	O.C. 82nd Bde. Hospl.	Nil.
2945 Pte. McHugh J.	MUMPS. Adm. 82nd Bde. Hospl. 7/3/15.	do	Nil.
2027 Pte. Lees W.	INFLUENZA. Adm. 82nd Bde. Hospl. 7/3/15.	do	Nil.
593 Pte. McGarrigle W.	LUMBAGO. Adm. 82nd Bde. Hospl. 7/3/15.	do	Nil.
2346 Pte. Murdoch D.	B.W. RIGHT BUTTOCK. Adm. 82nd Bde. Hospl. 8/3/15	do	Nil.
2246 Pte. Guilder L.	RHEUMATISM. Adm. 82nd Bde. Hospl. 11/3/15.	do	Nil.
990 Sgt. Paton A.	BULLET WOUND R. BIG TOE. Adm. 81st Amb. 7/3/15.	O.C. 81st Field Amb.	Nil.

G.H.Q.,
26/3/15.

Captain,
I/C Infantry Records, 3rd Echelon,

1/9th Battn: Arg: & Sutherlamd Highlanders.

MONTHLY RETURN OF BURIAL PLACES OF N.C.O's & MEN OF THE ABOVE UNIT FOR THE MONTH OF MARCH.

NIL.

~~S-H-Q-~~,
30/3/15.
                                Captain,
                  I/C T.F. Infantry Records, 3rd Echelon.

Casualti   No. 1 District.

1/9th. Bn, Argyll & Sutherland Highlanders.

Regl. No.	Rank & Name	Casualty	Rpd. by.	Prev. Rpd. Casualty.
593	Pte. McGarrigle	W. To Duty 25/3/15	O.C. Con. D. Rouen	S.
1573	Pte. Thomson	C. To Duty 25/3/15	do.	S.
2592	Pte. Moody	W. To Duty 27/3/15	do.	S.
2291	Pte. McFadyen	J. To Duty 21/3/15	O.C. Details, Boulogne.	S.
1830	Pte. Grant	G. To Duty 27/3/15	O.C. Con. D. Rouen	S.

Captain,

31/3/15   I/c., Terrl. Infantry Records, 3rd. Echelon, G.H.Q.

CASUALTIES AFFECTING OFFICERS:

1/9th Battn: Argyll & Sutherland Highrs.

Lieut:Belfrage A.G. WOUNDED BOTH LEGS, Adm.Hospital,21/3/15.TO DUTY, 13/4/15.
2/Lieut:Napier I.P.R. LUMBAGO, Adm.Hospital,21/3/15.TO DUTY, 15/4/15.
2/Lieut:Wright W.G. PLEURISY, Adm.Hospital,15/3/15.TO CONVALESCENT
                                                    HOME,NICE,20/3/15.

81st Inf.Bde.
27th Div.

1/9th BATTN. THE ARGYLL & SUTHERLAND HIGHLANDERS.

A P R I L

1 9 1 5

WAR DIARY or INTELLIGENCE SUMMARY

Army Form C. 2118.

(Erase heading not required.)

Place	Date	Hour	Summary of Events and Information	Remarks and references to Appendices
YPRES	April 1		Billeted in the town. Enemy aeroplanes working rather daringly over Sec Y.	
"	2		"	
"	3		"	
"	4	4 a.m.	Left in enemy aerial bombardment. DUMBARTON LAKE from the 88th Bde. Regs befor 17. (Gds.) Got in quite early for slight accident. 2 wounded.	
Hercuthage	5		H.Q. in trees near lake. Shelled in forenoon - one shell out shed by Hall. 8 casualties. 3 killed, 5 wounded.	
"	6		Visit of Brigadier. Tranches quiet: 2 killed, 3 wounded.	
"	7		In trenches - enfilade fire in 57. 2 killed, 4 wounded.	
"	8		Heavy fire in trench 57. Sous-Brigadier - Comdt'd Col Campbell 2nd Cameron - 1 killed. Relieved at 11 P.M. and left for Vlamertinghe.	
Vlamertinghe	9		Resting. Captain Guy (Adjutant) ordered to join HAVER RORKE. Captain Young Pl Adj. Pl. Adj. Lieut Lovitt duty Quartermaster.	
"			Lieut V.M.G. Menzies Lt. R.S. reported as Adjutant. Captain Young left. Posting draft of 50 new arrivals - of these it proves to be heavily drafted.	
"	10		Resting.	
"	11		Left 6.30 P.M. and marched to GLENCORSE WOOD where in relief of 4th R.S.	
"	12		Got in quietly. 1 wounded.	
GLENCORSE WOOD	13		Shelling. Visited by Brigadier General Ropes. 1 killed, 1 wounded.	

WAR DIARY
or
INTELLIGENCE SUMMARY.

(Erase heading not required.)

Army Form C. 2118.

Instructions regarding War Diaries and Intelligence Summaries are contained in F.S. Regs., Part II. and the Staff Manual respectively. Title pages will be prepared in manuscript.

Place	Date	Hour	Summary of Events and Information	Remarks and references to Appendices
GLENCORSE WOOD	14.		In wood. Visit of General Snow. Shelling of trenches. Ridiggio Communication trench. Shortage of sand bags.	1 man aviator in wounded himself
"	15.		In trenches. Wood heavily shelled.	
"	16.		Relieved by 9th R.S. 11 P.M. Marched to YPRES.	
YPRES	17.		Resting.	
"	18.		Resting.	1 man aviator in shell
"	19.		Relieving. Heavy shelling for 2 hours with large shells; companies in cellars — no casualties	
"	20.		Very heavy shelling. Committed Divisional Staff. Left 9.30 for Yser concentred cellars be relieved by 9th R.S.	2 men wounded enter dispersal in Ypres
	21		Good deal of shelling. One man killed in Dug-out.	
Glencorse Wood	22.		In wood. Shelled at intervals; in trenches improving trenches	
	23.		In wood. No things. Shelled. Improving trenches. One man killed; one wounded	Communication trench
	24.		In wood. Relief due; but did not come	3 wounded

WAR DIARY
or
INTELLIGENCE SUMMARY.
(Erase heading not required.)

Army Form C. 2118.

Place	Date	Hour	Summary of Events and Information	Remarks and references to Appendices
Glencorse Wood	25		Weather bad. Still in wood. Shelling continuous. No relief by Q.R.R. Relieved C Company from Bth trenches. Intik' trenches - in good condition. Killed 8 wounded	
"	26		In wood. Relief not effected. 30 men of draft arrived. 6 wounded	
"	27		B. relieved by A. Shelling. Adjutant upon the right shell burst also - 1 killed & wounded.	
"	28		Still in C, wood. No relief. Visited Brigade Surgent also Shooters of K.R.R. 1 killed 2 wounded Sen Brigade (HOOGE) got into their own trench line from firing	
"	29		Some shelling - Visited trenches. Now very strong- Communication	
"	30		trench complete. Relieving trenches to day owed to rain.	for month K 15 W 58

James Clark Lt Col.
Comdg 9th Arg & S. Highlanders

The,
    Command Paymaster,
    Rouen.

    The undermentioned casualties affecting Officers of the 1/9th Battalion Argyll & Sutherland Highlanders are forwarded for your information.

G.H.Q.,
2/4/15.

H Codrington

                                Captain,
I/C T.F. Infantry Section, 3rd Echelon.

Rank & Name.	Casualty.	By whom reported.	Prev.Rept.
2nd Lieut. Wright W.G.	On PLEURISY, adm. N Stn. Hospl. 15/3/15. Transf. to Conv. Home, Nice 20/3/15.	O.C. No.7 Stn. Hospl.	Nil.
2nd Lieut. Napier I.P.R.	LUMBAGO. adm. No. 4 Gen. Hospl. 23/3/15.	O.C. NO 4 Gen. Hospl.	Nil.
Lieut. Belfrage A.G.	G.S.W. LEGS. adm. No 4 Gen. Hospl. 23/3/15.	O.C. No.4 Gen. Hospl.	Nil.

1/9th Battalion Argyll & Sutherland Hrs.

7. (War)

3rd Echelon.
3/4/15.

1.	STRENGTH:	2nd Lieut. Birrell G.W.C.		Embarked Southampton, 18/3/15 Joined Battn: 23/3/15.
2.	Death	No.14 Cpl. McKay	G. A.	Died of wounds 20/3/15.
3.	Transfers.	1831 Pte. McNally	R. D.	Transferred to England 25/3/15. (ship not stated)
		1921 Pte. Blackwood	W. C.	Transferred to England 26/3/15 per H.S. Oxfordshire.

Captain,
I/C T.F. Infantry Records, 3rd Echelon, 3/4/15.

Casualty Report.   **No. District.**

1/9th Battn: Argy & Suthld: Highlrs:

Regtl.No.Rank&Name	Casualty	By whom reported	Prev.Rept.
14 Cpl.McKay G.	DIED OF WOUNDS, 20/3/15	O.C. Battalion.	Nil.
1817 Pte.McBride D.	TO DUTY, 28/3/15	O.C. Convl.Depot	S.
1572 Pte.Scott J.	TO DUTY, 23/3/15	O.C. Base Details	S.

G.H.Q.,
7/4/15.

Hodrington
Captain,
I/C T.F. Infantry Records, 3rd Echelon

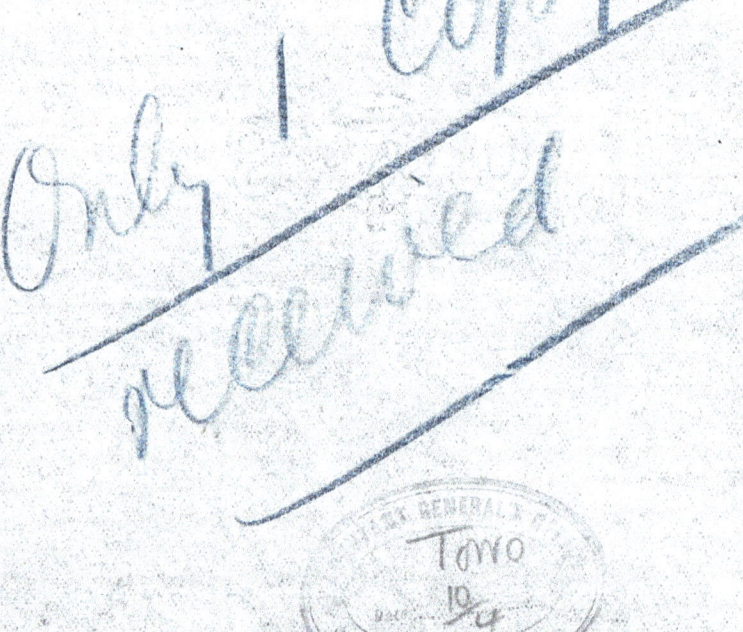

Only 1 copy received

Casualty Report.   No. 1 District.

1/9th Battalion Argyll & Suth. Hrs.

Regl.No.	Rank & Name.	Casualty.	By whom reptd.	Prev. Rept.
2059	Pte. Richardson J.	KILLED IN ACTION 5/4/15.	O.C. Battalion	Nil.
2011	Pte. McLachlin M.	KILLED IN ACTION 5/4/15.	,,	Nil.
2512	Pte. Colquhoun J.	KILLED IN ACTION 7/4/15.	,,	Nil.
1711	Pte. Russell A.	KILLED IN ACTION 8/4/15.	,,	Nil.
1061	Cpl. McNair J.	KILLED IN ACTION 6/4/15.	,,	Nil.
2565	L.Cpl. Johnstone W.	DIED OF WOUNDS 6/4/15.	,,	Nil.
714	Pte. Beaton C.	DIED OF WOUNDS 7/4/15.	,,	Nil.
2593	Pte. Munro D.	DIED OF WOUNDS 8/4/15.	,,	Nil.
1393	L.Cpl. Logan M.	TO DUTY, 23/3/15.	O.C.Conv.Depot	W.
2027	Pte. Lees W.	TO DUTY, 15/3/15.	O.C.82nd Bde.Hospl.	S.
1337	Pte. L.Cpl. Graham R.	TO DUTY, 6/3/15.	O.C.Conv.DEPOT.	S.
1771	Pte. Ralston A.	TO DUTY, 2/4/15.	,,	S.

3rd Echelon,
15/4/15.

Officer I/C Territorial Infantry Records,
General Headquarters.

Lieut.Colonel,

Casualty Report.   No. I District.
         I/9th Battn. Argyll & Suth. Highrs.

Regtl.No.	Rank & Name	Casualty	By whom reported	Prev.Rept.
2166	Private Raeside J.	SEPTIC FOOT. R. TOE Adm. 83rd F.Amb. 23/3/15.	O.C. 83rd F.Amb.	Nil
2556	" Hall A.	BLISTERED HEELS. Adm. 83rd F.Amb. 23/3/15	do	Nil
2635	" Potter D.J.	SPRAINED LEFT ANKLE Adm. 83rd Fd.Amb 23/3/15	do	Nil
2440	" Thomson W.	SEPTIC R. KNEE Adm. 83rd Fd. Amb. 23/3/15	do	Nil
864	Sergeant Swan T.	INFLUENZA Adm. 83rd Fd.Amb 23/3/15	do	Nil
1800	Corporal McInnes D.	INFLUENZA AdM. 83rd Fd. Amb 23/315	do	Nil
1247	Private Watson A.	BLISTERED L. HEEL AdM. 83rd Fd. Amb. 23/3/15	do	Nil

Woodrington Captain.
                                i/c T.F. Infantry Records, 3rd Echelon.

17/4/15.

Casualty Report.   No. 1 District.

1/9th Battn: Argyll & Suth: Hrs.

Regtl.No. Rank & Name.		Casualty.	By whom Reported	Prec. Rept.
1567 Pte. McNeill	D.	TO DUTY, 13/4/15.	O.C.Conv.Depot.	W.
2571 Pte. Kennedy	D.	TO DUTY, 16/4/15.	,,	S.
2327 Pte. Ferguson	A.	TO DUTY, 17/4/15.	,,	S.
778 L.Cp&Borland	W.	TO DUTY.(Class B)17/4/15.	,,	W.
1620 Pte. Moodie	C.C.	COLIC.Adm.N.M.Div. C.C.Stn.30/3/15.	O.C.N.M.Div.C.C. Stn.	Nil.
96 Cpl. Brown	S.M.	G.S.W.LEFT ARM& Trans.O.C.,H.S."Valdivia" to England per H.S. "Valdivia"		W.

G.H.Q.,
20/4/15.

                                                      Captain,
                    Officer I/C T.F.Infantry Records.

Casualty Report.   No. 1 District.

1/9th Battn: Argyll & Suthd: Hrs.

Rgtl.No.	Rank & Name.		Casualty.	By whom Reported.	Prev.Rpt.
23	Pte.Drummond	J.	TO DUTY, 8/4/15.	O.C.Conv. Depot.	
06	Pte.McLachlan	H.	TO DUTY, 8/4/15.	do	
23	Pte.Scott	J.	TO DUTY, 10/3/15.	O.C.81st Field Amb.	
67	Pte.McLean	A.	TO DUTY, 24/3/15.	O.C.No.9 Stn.Hospl.	
47	Pte.Hunter	J.L.	MYALGIA, adm.84th Field Amb.5/4/15.	O.C.84th F.Amb.	Nil.
44	Pte.Gilfillan	S.	INFLUENZA.adm.84th Field Amb.5/4/15.	do	Nil.
69	Pte.Forbes	D.	INFLAMED L&KNEE,adm. 84th Field Amb. 5/4/15.	do	Nil.
99	Pte.Halkett	T.	INFLUENZA,adm.84th Field Amb.5/4/15.	do	Nil.
23	Pte.Dick	W.	INFLUENZA,adm.84th Field Amb.5/4/15.	do	Nil.
21	Pte.Ferrie	J.	INFLUENZA,adm.84th Field Amb.5/4/15.	do	Nil.

.H.Q.,
5/4/15.

Officer I/C T.F.Infantry Records.

Captain,

www.ingramcontent.com/pod-product-compliance
Lightning Source LLC
Chambersburg PA
CBHW081249170426
43191CB00037B/2092